I0479573

HOW TO DOMINATE YOUR MARKET IN ONE YEAR OR LESS

*FOR REAL ESTATE AGENTS ONLY

4 STEPS TO CREATE AN AUTOMATIC SUPPLY OF NEW LEADS COMING IN WEEK AFTER WEEK

By Will Cunningham

Copyright © 2020 OverForkOver LLC

All rights reserved.

All rights reserved. No part of this publication may be reproduced, distributed, or transmitted in any form or by any means, including photocopying, recording, or any other electronic or mechanical methods, without the prior written permission of the publisher, except in the case of brief quotations embodied in critical reviews and certain other non-commercial uses permitted by copyright law. For permission requests, contact the publisher at betteragentacademy.com.

ISBN: 978-1-6542-7206-7

DEDICATION

I would like to dedicate this book to my mentor Clay Dickens.
Without your guidance and expertise, I would still be struggling –
thank you.

CONTENTS

WHY I WROTE THIS BOOK

Like many people, I struggled for years with the ups and downs in the market, stressing over every deal, not knowing what marketing I should do, not knowing what worked when I did any marketing, and not knowing how to really get any referrals. I joined referral networks, joined the Chamber of Commerce, I sat on volunteer boards, spent a ton of time and energy, and it didn't produce more business – not really. Yes, I got some referrals, but totally untargeted, most people I couldn't help, and it was just so frustrating. If you know what I am talking about, then you are in the right place, keep reading!

But then things changed for me when I went to work for someone I had known for a few years – a very successful guy. As his assistant, I learned how to position myself as an expert, where to focus my marketing for maximum results, and how to get qualified, real referrals, ready and eager to work with me. Which is where I have been operating for years now, every day new referrals calling me, wanting to work with me, even bugging me when I tell them no. I will give you all the details very soon on how to do this.

However…

I am actually a lender, not a Real Estate agent. I have my CA DRE Broker's License, #1300440. I got it in 2002, but I have always worked as a residential lender. For most of my career I have worked for a local bank writing residential mortgage loans. In the last 25 years, I have closed thousands of transactions, and worked with hundreds of Real Estate agents. I've seen some great agents, and some awful ones, but I found that extremely few follow even some of the ideas in this book – which is why I wrote this book…to help Real Estate agents just like you become more successful.

DISCLAIMER

It wouldn't be any fun without a disclaimer...

Here's mine: Licensed Real Estate Agents Only!

I need to say that this one-of-a-kind training is only for licensed Real Estate Agents, Residential or Commercial, who have been working full time at this for at least one year. You need to have closed some deals and this must be your main business, and your main source of income. You should also want more referrals, more deals, and better marketing. And I need to point out that this will benefit veteran agents and beginners alike.

No guarantees of results, just of your satisfaction

Of course, this is Real Estate, so there are no guarantees on results for you specifically, and I cannot state that you will make any more money, or any claims like that. That is all up to you and how much effort and work you put into this, just like everything in life, right?

However, I can guarantee you will be happy with what you learn, and I am very confident that you have not heard everything I have to teach you in this book. I have never seen even one agent out there do everything in this blueprint, and only a handful of the agents even do a few of these things, so this is not mainstream training, far from it.

One thing: make sure to run everything you do, and every idea you take action on, by your broker and government authority in your state. Make sure everything you do complies with RESPA (Real Estate Settlement Procedures Act). So, make sure to check with your State Governing Agency or Department on your referral activities.

.

STEP ONE – MINDSET

Step One is all about getting the right Mindset. Like building a house, you need to first pour a strong foundation. This first step is just like pouring a strong foundation, but for the rest of your career. Hopefully, you already have a lot of this figured out, but I strongly suggest you take this step seriously. Please invest in yourself by reflecting on how you think about and approach your work and the people you work with.

Here is the point: You must think differently than your competition in order to stand out and get noticed, and by doing this you will have clients chasing you, instead of you chasing them. Please read that again. Dominating your market starts with thinking differently than other agents, then doing things they are not doing. But this means doing the right things.

Wouldn't you agree that being successful and doing the right things over and over all begin with your beliefs and what you think on a daily basis? Well, with Step One you get your head in the right place and if you do that then the rest is much easier. Easier because your thinking and beliefs are a match with your daily actions.

Now, you could certainly be successful just by taking action on what is in this book, but I put this step first for a reason. So, I'll repeat: You must think differently than your competition in order to stand out and get noticed, and by doing this you will have clients chasing you, instead of you chasing them.

Before we go any further, consider downloading the workbook and get access to the video training I've put together for you. Just visit this website: betteragentacademy.com – these tools are free, and they will help guide you through this material. The benefit for you is that when you read the book, listen to, and watch the videos, and write down your thoughts and ideas, you will start putting your marketing plan together automatically.

Ok, let's dive in!

PART ONE: DESERVING SUCCESS

To be successful, you need to deserve success. Meaning, success in any endeavor is not an accident and it doesn't happen just because you may be a nice person. In this case, I define success as being the "go to" expert, being sought out by buyers and sellers, and being a dominate force in your market. Well, this will not happen unless you deserve it. What I mean, and what you need to understand deep down in the core of who you are, is that this success will only come by doing the things that bring this success – and not just doing them once, but over and over and over again.

You can't just show up ready for work, treat people well, close deals with a smile, and expect to get a ton of referrals. That's what most Real Estate agents do and that's why most agents struggle.

2

HOW TO DOMINATE YOUR MARKET

To dominate your market you must do more, and you must be consistent. Understand this right out of the gate and embrace it – you need to go above and beyond to be successful at Real Estate. You must stand out. The good news is that it does not take that much to stand out and get a lot of referrals. You just need to have some new knowledge, get a plan together, and work the plan consistently.

Speaking of referrals...I need to point something out that bothers me about some of the agents that I've worked with: Deserving more referrals, and therefore more success, means that you must EARN the referrals. Many agents just don't deserve to be referred to buyers or sellers...they don't do what it takes to deserve them.

Think about this: if some friends of yours came into town, and before meeting up with you, they wanted to go grab some breakfast first. They ask you to recommend a place to eat – are you going to recommend a place that's dirty? Or has horrible service? Or has terrible food? No way. But why? It's because their experience will reflect upon you because you suggested the place to them. Their good or bad experience is partly dependent on your recommendation. You must consider this when asking for referrals from your clients and the public at large. No one just refers a Real Estate Agent because they are good looking, or because that's what they do for a living. You must earn referrals – be the agent that people trust to take care of anyone who they refer to you.

Now, how do you do this? Here's how...

PART TWO: BE CUSTOMER FOCUSED

Next, you need to shift your mindset to being customer focused. Putting the client first, their needs, their goals, their success – this is how you earn future business.

No one will recommend an agent that they know will not have the interests of the client in mind, or a priority. Out of the dozens of agents that I work with on a consistent basis, only a few do I recommend. This is specifically due to how they treat their clients - the buyers and sellers they're helping.

This is so simple, yet many agents I have worked with don't do this. I have seen agents push for a quick closing, push for an offer at any price, even avoid taking their client's calls. While some clients can be difficult to work with, if you don't work for their best interest then it will show. And realize this: more than just your clients are watching. The lender, escrow officer, appraisers, and even other agents see how you treat other people and they will decide to refer you business or not on how you treat your clients. Remember this, it's super important.

If you already do this, great! You are ahead of your competition. If not, then shift now out of making decisions that mean getting the deal closed at all cost, getting the maximum commission, etc. When you do this, your customers (and by the other parties involved in the deal) see it and feel it and they know you don't have their best interest in mind. It gives them a reason NOT to send you more business.

PART THREE: RELATIONSHIP VS. TRANSACTIONAL

Real Estate is transactional in most cases. You help a buyer buy a property, or a seller sell a property. Once that's completed you move on to the next deal, right? Well you must stop thinking this way. You must now realize that your next deal will come from the relationships that you build. Therefore, your focus must be on building relationships instead of just getting the deal closed (and you paid). If you do this correctly, then one relationship can be worth many, many deals. Stop focusing on the finish line and start building a business – one relationship at a time.

Who are you building relationships with? Everyone. Everyone involved directly, and indirectly, within the whole industry should know:

1) Who you are

2) The market you serve

3) And completely trust you to do a great job

This is what you are working towards. Keep this in mind when you are closing your deals.

How do you do this? Well, this is about your mind set. So, for now, just know that this is a goal. At every opportunity take small steps to cultivate a relationship with other people at some level. You don't need to go overboard or be cheesy, like giving everyone your business card and asking them if they know anyone who is looking to buy or sell – I run from those agents and most people do. No, instead just start with being friendly and genuinely interested in them. Ask them questions and work to find some common ground. This is sales 101, and agents generally miss this great opportunity because they are just working to finish the transaction and get paid.

So, from now on, everyone you come in contact with treat them with a smile, a hello, and (if appropriate) ask them "what do you do?" and "how did you get into the business?", etc. This will naturally lead them to ask you back what you do. Remember to stand out and be memorable just be interested in them first. Admit it, people who show interest in you will stand out and you'll remember them...am I right? This is basic human nature, so use it to help build a stronger connection.

This is also the best way is to find some common interests. These are anchors that a person would use for their own reference (like kids, type of car, hobbies, where you grew up, etc.).

Be a good listener and ask a lot of questions. This gets people to open up to you. Everyone loves talking about themselves most of the time. If you find someone that is not interested in talking, try asking them their opinion on a piece of advertising, or something like that. Remember to be yourself and be natural. You don't need to pretend.

PART FOUR: YOU MUST EARN THEIR TRUST

You should see by now how these are all connected, right? This is all about building and earning Trust. No one will refer you clients, or hire you, if you don't build trust. This is not new, I know many of you have been told this, but do you do it? What is your plan to build trust in the public eye, or your client's eye? No one refers a person (or company) they don't trust. If your mindset revolves around earning trust, building relationships, helping your client with their needs first, and consistently taking action on the tasks that are needed to deserve success, then you will be successful in this business – that's the bottom line.

PART FIVE: SCHEDULE IMPORTANT TASKS

We're not quite done with the mindset step yet. You also need to be great at time management. This is not as scary as it sounds. The simple and effective way to get your time under control and get more done is to plan and schedule the important tasks. Get a calendar, use your smart phone, computer, or whatever you want and whatever is easy for you. But do it – everyday.

Here is a simple idea - Start every workday with your calendar out in front of you.

1)Review the plan for that day, then...

2) Review the week, and then...

3) Review the month.

This keeps the important tasks up front and center.

Have on your schedule a day each month, or maybe one day a week where you have set aside an hour to plan and review your month and your year goals. Then schedule your marketing, your training and education, and your relationship building. The idea here is to get you to start planning and putting down on paper or computer when you will have time to do those important things that will be required if you are to be the go-to person in your market.

If you are like me, then if it is not scheduled, then the chances of it getting done are slim. But I find that if I book the time then the task ends up being less stressful and gets completed.

Now, I am not referring to every task, just the important ones that you need to be consistent at. Here is the list:

- Planning your marketing

- Executing on your marketing

- Building/reinforcing key relationships

- Furthering your education

- And scheduling your day, week, month

- Finally, goal setting – setting and reviewing

If you already are a schedule type person, great, you should know how much more productive you are when you are consistent with your planning. And if you are not already scheduling or planning your time, then I think you might be pleasantly surprised at how helpful this can be. And it really does not take much time, a few minutes a day, to an hour a week is all that is needed.

Part Six: Your Job Is Marketing

The last part in Step One is this important clarification: Your real job is marketing.

While it is true that the money ends up in your pocket by closing a deal, your job is actually marketing. If you work and focus on marketing, then the deals will flow to you naturally and easily. This is a very important distinction that will separate the regular agents with the very successful ones.

Marketing includes the normal tasks of sending out mailings, etc., but also includes building relationships, and positioning yourself as an expert. All this is covered in the coming chapters. The point is, you must shift your thinking to the belief and understanding that your job is marketing yourself properly. That's it. Yes, you need to meet with clients, deals will need to be negotiated, contracts signed, escrows opened, etc., I get that, and Yes, sometimes they can consume your whole day. But here is the thing...ANY agent can do that. What will set you apart is the real work, the work that ultimately will get you a ton of business - and that is marketing (doing the things I teach in this book) consistently. The payoff will be huge once you understand this.

STEP TWO – TARGET MARKET

Step One showed you some ideas to help you think and approach how you do things differently. Hopefully, it made you a little uncomfortable. Like Grant Cardone says, you need to get uncomfortable to make any progress. Meaning, just like a muscle, only when you are pushed out of your comfort zone will you really grow. This next step may be uncomfortable for you, but I promise, it is a game changer.

Step two is about picking a specialty. You absolutely do not want to be one of those agents who can help everyone. Those agents are afraid of losing out on a deal, but what you need to realize is that:

By not having a specialty, you actually are saying there is nothing special about you.

So, how do you become special? Start with focusing on a niche, or target market. But first, let's break down the categories of a target market. This will help you come up with your perfect fit.

A target market can be in one of three categories:

- Property Type

- Area

- Client Situation

PART ONE: PROPERTY TYPE

A target market can be a type of property, like condos, ranch property, view homes, mobile homes, beach or lake front, vacation rentals, equestrian (horse) properties, even historic homes, etc. For you commercial agents: retail, warehouse, apartments, office, etc.

Now think about your geographical region – the broad area you are located in. What kind of properties are there in your area? Lots of condos or apartments? Or lots of ranches? Luxury homes? Waterfront? Or maybe mobile homes? Now think if there is a gap in the servicing of these properties. For instance, in the area I live in, there are a ton of luxury estates, very high end. And there are a lot of ranch and equestrian properties. Through my experience, there are many more agents who target the luxury market than ranch and equestrian. If I wanted to target one of these, I would go after the Ranch and Equestrian property market.

Sometimes there are properties that are unique because they are located near a college, or airport, etc. Drill down into sub-niche properties if needed.

Now please write down in the workbook or in a notebook: List out all the types of properties in your area. What type of property are you comfortable with? What do you have experience with? And, then, what types of properties are underserved by agents in your area now (meaning there are no agents who specialize in these properties)?

HOW TO DOMINATE YOUR MARKET

PART TWO: AREA

Another target market category is a geographical area, like a neighborhood. Areas will have common types of properties, for the most part, but the difference would be the location. A single-family home in one area may have different buyers and sellers compared to another single-family in another area. In my market there are many of these distinct and separate neighborhoods, and each can command a different type of buyer and seller. Some have different types of properties, like more ranches and luxury, while others have more mobile homes, and others have more waterfront. I think you get the idea. But the point is that while one area may have waterfront homes, there are probably other areas that also have waterfront homes, but the feeling of the areas differs. Maybe you have some expertise in or live in a neighborhood that can be your target market?

Start writing down all the areas/neighborhoods in your geographic area. Maybe start with the high-end and work towards the low-end priced properties. Make sure you include distinctions like historic homes, larger lots, mixed use, etc. Then, start thinking about your knowledge and expertise in any of these areas, and then your desire for learning more about any one of them.

Here is a good example of an area for your target market: In the city where I grew up, Santa Barbara, CA, there is an area called the "Upper East". I always thought an agent should position themselves as the expert for that area. The Upper East of Santa Barbara is about twelve blocks long, and about six blocks wide. It is mostly historic homes, with some extensively remodeled homes as well. Prices are $1.5 million to around $5 million. Buyers for this area are specific. They usually already know they want to buy there. A great way to position yourself for this specific market would be to knock on every door over a few months period of time, introducing yourself to EVERY homeowner. Tell them you specialize in their neighborhood

11

(using the name of the area, like Upper East for instance). It's best if you also live there, or work there, but you can still stand out if you don't yet.

The idea is to think about the specific areas in the over-all geographical area you serve and see if there is any that you'd like to dominate. Write down all the physical areas in your over-all location. List out the neighborhoods that have different feels, or physical barriers, etc. Start thinking about which ones may be a good target market for you.

PART THREE: CLIENT SITUATION

Finally, there are different types of people that you can help. Meaning, people in certain situations. For instance, first time homebuyers, divorcing couples, seniors, second home/vacation home buyers, investors, distressed sellers, affluent buyers, or even buyers who need help in another language. Continue adding to your notes: Think of who you would like to help, and who fits your ideal client. Are there types of situations that you gravitate towards? Have you been in a similar situation, and so you can relate to these people?

Maybe there is a large company that is planning on relocating to your area? They may then have out of the area buyers who need your help. Or maybe there is already a large employer who needs help finding quality homes for its staff? Or, maybe you are in an area where there are a lot of retiring seniors who need an expert help them buy the right home (smaller home, or one with no or very small yard, easy access, etc.)? Perhaps you once helped a seller facing foreclosure and you were really satisfied with finding a solution that helped? Think about this, and specifically about the over-all area you serve. I can tell you that in my area, there are employers who need help with their employees to find affordable housing, and there are many very wealthy, second homeowners, etc. However, there are always divorcing couples who need help in every area.

Having a target market that is a group of people in a certain situation can be great, you just need to really enjoy working with and helping these people. Understanding their motivations and the other factors in their lives helps, for instance being patient with a seller facing foreclosure, or being flexible with your work hours with out of town clients, etc. Also, this is a great category of target market for referrals from other industries and so working with other businesses should be interesting to you. More on this later!

PART FOUR: WHO IS YOUR IDEAL CUSTOMER?

Hopefully by now you have some idea on a target market that makes sense for you. Now think about your ideal customer. Who do you want to help? Or who are you really good at dealing with? Start thinking about this. Go grab a coffee and sit down with a pen and some paper. I want you to write down the times when you did a great job and you really enjoyed the work. Was it because the client? The property? The situation? Reflect on what you are good at in your job, and what you enjoy. Write down the top three to five instances that come to mind and keep this to refer back to.

You need to come up with a target market, here's why. No Real Estate Agent can help everyone. And no agent will be great at all types of buyers and sellers, all types of properties, and all types of situations, etc. The HUGE, glaring error most of the agents I see struggling out there right now, is that they are trying to be everything to everyone, and they end up being barely noticed by anyone. Remember, by not having a specialty, you are not special (at least not in the eyes of those who can refer you business). If you think that you can help everyone, then you need to stop now. This thinking is based in fear and you need to realize how much this is hurting you, right now, today. The fear is of losing out on new business. When, in reality, you are demonstrating a lack of confidence that your potential clients pick up on. No one wants to work who is desperate. Yet, most everyone likes to work with an expert.

PART FIVE: WRAP UP

Now let's put this all together. So far, you should have written down some types of properties that you gravitate towards, some areas in your city or county that are ideal for you, and then some situations where you are more comfortable with. It's a good time to review your notes.

It may be obvious to you right away, or maybe not so easy to determine, but what is your target market going to be? Sometimes one of the categories above is so big in your area, that you need to overlay another of the categories on top. For instance, let's say that your city has many, many condo projects, too many for one agent to effectively dominate all of them. So, overlay another category of target market, like location: Condos in the North end of the city let's say, or only higher priced condo complexes in the city (therefore an affluent clientele).

In the workbook or your notebook, list out your top 3 ideas. Maybe they are all helping wealthy clients, but you are just not sure about the area, or the type of property? Or, maybe you are very knowledgeable about mobile homes, but you are not interested in working with seniors or first-time home buyers? Now is the time to dig deep into this and figure out what is the best fit for you.

At this point, I suggest you let this all sink in. Maybe have some discussions with other agents, friends, family – not about what they think you should do, but just about the different types of properties in your geographic region, the neighborhoods and how they are all different (or similar), and then also about the types of situations when people buy and sell homes. What are pros and cons of each one? Just have some discussions and do some thinking. The idea being: you need to determine how to stand out in a very noisy, crowded world. Picking a specialty is important, but changing it later is not ideal (could be very hard to do), so make sure to take the time to make the best decision possible.

Here is another example:

Let's say you look at your over-all area and decide that there are lots of condos. You have always noticed that condos sell well and there seem to be plenty of buyers and sellers, and you think you'd like to make that your specialty - your target market.

You live in a large city, and it is not practical for you to help clients in the far north area of your city, so you decide that mid-town to the very far reaches of the southern end will be your target market. Buyers and sellers of condos in this market will know who to go to – YOU!

Think about, and do some research if needed, on what the concerns of these buyers and sellers would be. Crime rates? Traffic congestion? Schools? These are very important, but also common for good agents to have as information readily available. But you are different, you make a point of walking each condo property in your target market twice a year, or more, and you attend at least one board meeting a year, or more for each condo property. You schedule a phone call or lunch with each HOA president and catch up on the property once every six months. You make a binder on each property for your office and you keep the current rules and regulations, CC&Rs, and maybe even the corporate by-laws in this binder. You know the rules of each property for pets, renting, etc. You work closely with 2-3 lenders who also specialize in condos in your area. Become friends with the Police Chief or Sherriff and speak to them regularly about the crime rates, schools, traffic accidents, etc. anything that a buyer would want to know.

Something like this has the direct benefit of educating you, so you can be best prepared to help your clients. But the indirect benefit is that the people you seek out and speak with regarding these properties will get to know you, and they will see that you are out there to help people. They will naturally refer you when asked about an agent who deals with condos. They won't even need to think about it, it'll be automatic.

Remember: The point is to set yourself apart from your competition. Think about why your clients would want to work with you instead of some other agent? What will you do differently? Your answer will make all the difference.

STEP THREE – BE THE EXPERT

Step Three is very important...this is where you own it. Be the Expert!

You can't do this without a target market. No one will believe you if you are an expert in all types of Real Estate everywhere, for all kinds of people, right? So, this is about positioning yourself to be perceived as the go-to person for your niche or target market – the expert they can count on for results.

A couple of things I want to say:

1) Almost every day I get a phone call where the person calling says something like: Do you lend on mobile homes? And I say: That's all I do. Once they here that they start listening more, paying close attention. They know they're talking to an expert simply because I told them that I specialize in that kind of loan. What did I do? Not much, but I immediately set myself apart from any other lender out there. So, it is not that hard to position yourself as an expert.

2) Remember that everyone on the planet was born with no previous

experience. We all started with no knowledge or experience. So, don't get down on yourself if you are starting with basically no knowledge or experience. Just start.

PART ONE: CLAIM IT

First you must claim it. This means decide fully that you are or will become the top expert for your target market – period! This starts in your head, but quickly becomes common knowledge out in the world. You don't need to go to school or pass a test that states you are now an expert at whatever you study.

Answer this: who is/was the greatest boxer of all time?

Many people will answer Muhammad Ali. I am sure this can be debated and argued, but why would many people choose him? It's because he claimed it. And not just once or twice, but for many, many years, and in all different situations he'd say: "I am the greatest!". Yes, he was a really good boxer! One of the best probably, but the greatest?

Can you imagine his legacy being as huge if he hadn't repeated that declaration again and again? And remember that he said this way before ever really being great, or even close to the greatest boxer ever. He said it to demonstrate where he was headed. This convinced himself as much as convincing the world. He had to believe it fully to be able to convince others.

So, claim it – say "I do this, this is who I am". For instance, "I am Chicago's top expert on duplexes, I help every-day folks become financially independent by helping them buy two family units for positive cash flow". This would be your USP (see part six below). And when you say it, believe it. It will feel strange at first but keep

18

doing it. Say it 100 times a day for a month or more. Own it!

PART TWO: GET GREAT

Essentially, to be the expert, you must be really, really, really good and very knowledgeable about your subject in order to convince people of your expertise and ability to help them. For anyone to have your name come up automatically in their head about which agent they should recommend when it comes to divorces, for example, they must have been previously convinced that you are the expert. You convince them by showing them. Demonstrating that you know more about your target market. Go the extra mile.

This is not about calling yourself what you are not. It is about getting good – really good – and then dominating. So, if you have decided that you are the next beach/lake front home expert in your town, or the top expert on view homes in a high-end, exclusive neighborhood, then do the research and study the market in depth. Look up the statistics and start keeping detailed files. Know each street, know each home. Look up the public records and get really good at what your buyers want, what your sellers want, what the city or county rules are, what projects will be happening in that area, etc. Meet the people who drive that market. Talk to them frequently about your niche.

PART THREE: PUBLISH

This is where things get exciting! I have not mentioned this before because it needs its own section and, yes, it's that important. This part and the next one are very powerful. If you JUST did one of these two things, you would see a lot more business come in.

It's easy to underestimate the power of writing a book or report on your target market... don't do that. Being a published author commands the respect of the public that will set you apart from your competition.

Now, don't panic. This is easier than you think. It doesn't have to be 300 pages and published by a huge company, in fact, I don't suggest wasting time down that road. There are many other ways to get a printed book completed. And even a 20 page report about the top 10 worst mistakes when buying a beach/lake front home in your city will set you apart and do the job.

Here is what you need to do: come up with the top 3 -10 things your target audience should never do – things that are specific to them (things that someone in your target market may experience or consider but should avoid).

Or approach it from the other end, such as the 5 most important questions a young family should ask when buying their first home, for example. The point is that it's fairly easy to come up with 3 or more important points that your target market will face, and you need to guide people to a solution, before they can even ask, before they even know it's important to them. This shows that you are helping them and that you know what you're doing. It shows you've done this before, and it paints you as the expert.

Maybe you have enough knowledge now and your target market has enough useful information about it for buyers and sellers to get some real benefit out of a hundred page book, but more than likely it is just a simple report, again just a few pages will set you apart.

The key is that it must be useful, not fluff. And not generic information that you find about what schools are in the district, etc. Do not include information that most other agents can provide. Stand apart. For the condo example, it may be the 5 most important questions for a dog owner when buying a condo in Atlanta. I can think of many questions that this could include, I am sure you can too, but also make sure to answer those questions. For example, if you were to be helping dog owners in Atlanta (not saying that is a great target market), you would want to come up with the questions every dog owner would want to ask and then answer those as well. Like, what rules do local condo complexes have for dog owners? Then list all the condo complexes and their rules. Then point out why it's helpful to know this upfront.

This does not have to be complicated. Just do it. Have these reports printed on high-quality paper, maybe a hire a free-lance graphic artist to make it look really good. Come up with some branding, like a logo and specific colors. Maybe a tri-fold hand out. Come up with something that you can hand to your prospects that HELPS them and shows that you know your stuff. This will scream expert at them!

Another idea is to hire a college student to do some research on your target market. Have them determine the most important features, history, benefits, and drawbacks. For instance, if you are focusing on a historic area, then have them research the history and create a book around this information. Have a photographer (hopefully a student who needs the money and work) to photograph the historic homes in the research. I think you get the idea.

Here are some ideas for your target market:

Type of property: The top reasons why these properties are great, top things to look for when buying this kind of property; top things to avoid when buying this king of property; the top questions to ask when buying/selling this kind of property; etc.

If you're focusing on a situation then consider: How to buy a home when in divorce/retiring/your first home, etc.; what to avoid when buying/selling in this situation; etc.

And if your target market is an area, then consider: History of the area; reasons why living/owning here are awesome; etc.

Now, the topic does not have to be this direct, it could also be centered around something else than the act of buying or selling. Such as, the city as a whole, like why living in X City is awesome, or it could be centered around getting a loan, or home improvement, or hiring a moving company (like "how to get the best loan"; "the five words you need to say to any contractor to make them work on your home next"; "picking the best moving company in 3 easy steps"), etc. Remember the dog owners in Atlanta? Maybe connecting with the local veterinarian offices, pet shelters, mobile groomers, and even City government to help provide some information. Including a third party, like a lender, mover, contractor makes a lot of sense and has some hidden benefits (much more on working with 3rd parties in the next chapter!). First, you may lean on them for help in writing the material. Second, they may pay for some or all of it and want to give it out for their marketing as well. Just make sure you are the author, and if that means you must write it or pay for it (or both) then do it! Trust me, it's worth it.

The point of all of this is YOUR name as the author – passing out the info without you being the authority is worthless.

The title is just as important as the whole body and content. Stick to titles that obviously help your clients, like:

How to…

Top 3, 5, 10 benefits/things to look for/things to avoid/mistakes and how to avoid them/ways to lose money when buying/selling, etc.

The incredible history of….

Why buying/selling this kind of property right now makes sense...

I think you get the idea!

Just make sure it:

- Looks professional

- Helps the client

- Has an intriguing title

- And has you as the author

If you are no good at writing, then you could always hire a ghost writer, there is nothing wrong with that.

PART FOUR: EDUCATE

Another super important part of the marketing that 99% of agents are not taking advantage of – simply educating the public about their target market. That means having some outlet for educating people on your area of expertise and being available to answer their questions. For instance: Once a month having a free "how to get qualified to buy a beach/lake front home in your city" one hour seminar, or get on the radio for a half an hour show every week to answer callers questions, maybe a TV show, maybe write an article for your Sunday edition of the local paper.

The point is to get in front of people!

Go out there and educate the public. This does two things for you: First, you provide great, free info for your target customers which gives them an introduction to who you are and how you can help them, and second, it positions you as the expert. Who do you think they'll call? If you just spoke for half an hour and went through the mistakes to avoid when buying a home, do you think they'll want to work with you? Or will they go call some other agent?

This can tie in with your printed material. Your education maybe the same as what's in your booklet, but it doesn't have to be. You may want to just have a "come get qualified" seminar where you lead and sponsor the event. You can rotate your 3rd party contacts with a different one speaking about how they can help the audience. Just make sure that you are center stage always. You can speak for a few minutes about your target market and focus, then let them talk about their area of expertise, then you can wrap up and take questions.

Getting up in front of people positions you as the expert. Again, maybe an open to the public, once a month seminar for an hour where you talk about the benefits and drawbacks, and what to avoid, what to ask, etc. for your target market will do the job. This is the easiest in my opinion. Just find a popular space to meet, either pay for it, or negotiate a swap (more about this later), and then send out an invite to all the local newspapers, event calendars, TV, radio stations, area websites and blogs, etc. This is not hard and once you do one, the next will be easier.

Maybe a once-a-week radio show if your target market is fairly broad, or perhaps you can just be the Real Estate person, willing to talk about any topic, but you always mention your focus of course. Then perhaps TV, or printed articles on a regular basis.

But...you must do this consistently or it will all be a waste of time. The real benefit is conditioning the people in your city to know you as the go-to agent. They will not get this association until you've been doing this for many months. This is one of the most powerful marketing techniques out there and virtually no agents do this.

In fact, I firmly believe that any business that does not have leads coming in daily by word-of-mouth should do this immediately. The results are quick! And cheap!

Clients will hire you by your first seminar, and every seminar thereafter. But by the 4th or 5th time you do this, if you are marketing it well, then there will be people you don't know referring your name out as the agent to use.

One quick note, for those of you who have already written this off, probably because you just can't bring yourself to speak in front of a crowd, consider just contacting all the local news sources: TV, radio stations, local news casters, newspapers and other publications, local websites, etc. Just tell them that if they ever need an expert on Real Estate then they should contact you. You can give them your professional and expert opinion. This may help you overcome your stage fright by having them ask you questions vs. you coming up with what to talk about.

Ok, so just remember to:

- Get in front of people with quality information

- Do that over and over

PART FIVE: USP – UNIQUE SELLING PROPOSITION

Once you have determined what market you will target, and you start becoming an expert at that target market, you then need to come up with a USP. This stands for a Unique Selling Proposition. What is this? Think of it as your angle.

Here are some examples of a USP: Walmart = always a low price, Domino's Pizza = fast pizza, De Beers = diamonds for a relationship that will last forever, M&Ms = won't melt in your hands, etc. there are many more. You get the idea. What makes them unique? They say it right in their tag line...De Beers diamonds are forever. So, I suppose telling your spouse it's a De Beers diamond will convey that you want to be married forever to her, so that's more romantic.

But notice, these companies point out a benefit or feature, but they have just as many draw backs as any other company. I mean, a Volvo may be safe, but it's expensive as well. But their message isn't we're expensive, but we're worth it, their message is that their cars are very safe. There are actually LOTS of safe cars out there, but no other manufacturer has taken that approach. BMW is probably just as safe as Volvo, but BMW claims to be the Ultimate Driving Machine – for those who love to drive. It will be interesting to see how the self-driving trends of the future may or may not change this for them.

The point is: you need to separate yourself from your competition.

Your USP is part of that. Not only targeting a specific area, or type of situation, or type of property, but figuring out how you provide a specific benefit for your target market. Then TELL them...point it out.

A USP for you would be a simple sentence, or two, that tells anyone and everyone who you help and how you do that.

Think of it as one or two sentences that specifically state why people should hire you. And who you help, and how you do that. Here is an example: "I help downsizing seniors get top dollar for their current home, while helping them find the perfect, low maintenance mobile home to buy". Here is another one: "I help discerning, wealthy clients locate and acquire world-class equestrian estates". Basically, your USP tells the world your specialty, and by doing so, sets you apart from your competition.

It helps if put yourself in your clients' shoes. Think about who you are helping and what concerns they will have. List them out. Think about what problems they will face and make a list of them. Make sure to answer their questions before they can even ask them.

You see, 95% of agents out there don't do this. They assume the best way to get business is to just show up. When was the last time you saw an agent who did this, who had a specific tag line that said exactly who they help and how they do that?

Do this and you will set yourself apart. And this must clearly tell them what's the benefit for them.

Now is the time for you to come up with your own USP. You have thought about who you want to serve, now come up with your unique statement that tells the world why they should hire you – how can you help them?

STEP FOUR – MARKETING SYSTEM

This is your marketing system. Everything in this book, what we just went over. If you just did this every month consistently, and really focused on a specific target market to help – really made that niche your specialty - then you would be unstoppable and remarkably busy.

PART ONE: BRING IT ALL TOGETHER

This has been a lot of information, but I really hope you are excited about it by now. I hope you can see how even implementing just some of this will really help you. Remember, you don't have to do it all tomorrow. In fact, I go over more of that soon.

But first...let's summarize:

You need to start thinking differently.

- If you want to be successful, you need to think and do things that will cause your success. You need to deserve it by doing the work.

• Put your clients' needs first and solve their biggest problems.

• Remember that every client and any interaction you have is an opportunity to build a relationship (vs. just saying goodbye after the transaction is closed).

• Focus on earning trust.

Then start scheduling everything.

• Scheduling your education.

• And getting your marketing done consistently. Remember, you job is marketing.

Next, get a Target Market.

• Determine your best customer.

• Focus on a type of property, an area, or a type of client.

• Be special by specializing in a type of property, or an area, or a type of client situation.

Become the expert!

• Own it in your mind, your words, your actions. Never doubt it. Be super confident in your abilities to help in your area of expertise.

• Get great. Do the research, talk to influencers in your target market, sit in on meetings, walk your talk.

Time to educate.

•   Write a book or report on your niche. Hand it out regularly to every client and everyone you encounter for business.

•   Teach and offer education for free to your target market (seminar, TV, Radio, etc.). Get in front of people!

Come up with a USP.

•   Get a USP which is just your simple way of telling anyone and everyone who you help and how you help them.

Remember, picking a big enough target market is key, but so is knowing a lot about it. And, you must then position yourself as the expert by showing the public that you are the expert. You do this by doing the research, knowing the movers and shakers in the market you serve, and then by writing a booklet and hosting a free seminar about your focus every month.

PART TWO: BUDGET

Time to start working on your budget. I mean for money AND time. This can sound scary or boring to some people, so I don't want to lose you here.

Start thinking about how much money you can put towards these efforts, and mostly how much time you can budget for these tasks.

You will need to set aside a few hours a week, but not much more. And start small, meaning don't get overwhelmed by thinking you need to do all of these things immediately. I suggest looking at your normal week and seeing where you typically have some down time. The key here is to set this time as a must-do in your schedule. Let's say it's Thursday from 9am to noon. This could be the time where you review the contacts that you made that week, and you follow up with them. Then you either book the room for your seminar and brainstorm on the topic you will speak about. Or, if you still need to work on your target market, then get to work on that. Or do some research on the key people in that area. The point is, set aside a specific time, at least once a week, to focus on this marketing strategy. This is your time budget.

PART THREE: BUILD YOUR TEAMS

Next, it's time to Build your Teams. I mean two separate teams of partners: One is a team of other RE Agents, and another team of 3rd party businesses and individuals.

First, let's go over the idea of having a team of other agents. You should assume that your efforts will create a lot of business that may not fall into your target market. You could do one of two things: You can either bring other agents in under you and guide them, with agreeing on a split of the commission; or, work a referral deal out with agents not working directly under you.

Let's review each.

First, you can help guide other agents to this kind of marketing strategy and guide them, assuming they pick a different target market. Let's say you team up with another agent you work well with and like, and you both strongly identify with condos. And your city is large

31

HOW TO DOMINATE YOUR MARKET

enough to split in half. Each of you decide to take one half and make it your own, but you agree ahead of time on a deal where you split all listings, 50/50, but you also split the marketing efforts. You each author one booklet on the benefits of condo ownership, and you each work on a monthly seminar in a central location. You get the idea. You build a team of agents (one besides you, or many) that all work towards the same goal, but each have a specific specialty. That way, once a lead comes in, you can very confidently give it away as you know that you will still get paid on it. Here is another example from my world: there is a very successful agent in my target market of mobile homes. He works very well with seniors and specializes in those transactions. However, he partners with a successful agent on regular houses in our city. This allows him to focus on his specialty, but also take regular listings, but hand them to his partner who does the leg work. Together they do very, very well. And they market together as a team.

Now, I realize that this agent team concept is not new, and in fact, it is quite common. However, the twist is to have each agent specialize in a target market. Property type, situation of the buyer or the seller, or an area (which can all overlap).

However, this could also be more of an informal agreement to just "trade leads". Where you both just give the other agent leads that you get that are not a match to your target market. This may not be a great way to work, but it probably works well for some agents. Just don't rule it out.

Second, is your team of other referral sources that (here's the key) share your target market. This is where you build relationships with businesses and people who compliment your efforts. For instance, a local restaurant whose ideal customers live in your target market and meet the criteria for clients in terms of income, and demographics, etc. Like a steakhouse in an area that has a lot of retired folks.

HOW TO DOMINATE YOUR MARKET

Assuming you share this target market, you would want to build a relationship with the owner and manager of this restaurant. We'll go over soon how they can help you, but you should get the idea. Another example is for waterfront property where many of the residents owns a boat. Maybe you have not targeted boat owners specifically, but there are a lot of them in your target market. So, you build a relationship with the boat yard owner and manager, or the boat brokerage, or marina, or the yacht club. Perhaps the yacht club can host your seminar of once a month on the top 5 worst mistakes a property owner in the area can make when selling/buying.

Here is a list of REGULAR referral businesses for Real Estate (these are the 3rd party referral sources that agents typically think of):

Escrow/Title/Closing Attorney

Contractors and handyman services

Homeowner insurance agents

Moving companies

Termite/Pest removal companies

Lenders

Yes, you should have a very solid list of businesses and relationships built with all these important services, but these are for all types of Real Estate.

Here is the list of businesses you may not have thought of, but probably should IF they match your target market:

- Restaurants that cater to your types of buyers and sellers

- Specialty contractors and landscapers – high-end/full-service remodel and landscapers if you target wealthy clients/areas, pool inspection and leak detection if your target market typically buys and sells homes with pools and spas.

- Specialty Insurance Agents – maybe you find out, through your research of your target market, that many of the properties you will encounter are in flood zone, or hurricane/wind zone, etc. then working with an agency that specializes in this kind of insurance.

- Car Dealerships – either located in your target market area, or those who also cater to your type of client.

- Tax/CPA firms – these are good to work with when you specialize in a type of situation, like your clients typically are having accounting and tax issues when experiencing life changes that you target (retirement, young families/first time home buyers, moving into the area, divorce, foreclosure, investors, etc.)

- Attorneys – very similar to the previous, attorneys are great for when your clients are experiencing life changes.

- Cleaning Services – High-end for wealthy clients, specialty cleaning for investors, and ones located in your area.

- Gyms – if your clients are typically health conscious, or maybe seniors, young families if the gym has a day-care, or maybe your area is close to a university and your target market is students, etc.

- Pool Service companies – this is regular pool service companies, but also as mentioned the leak detection services if your target market has a lot of pools and spas, etc.

- Grocery delivery service and local markets – again, targeting the same clientele or same area as you

- Lenders – specific to your type of property, maybe for your type of situation

- Furniture companies and interior designers – matching in clientele

- Pre-Schools and Day Care Facilities – if a match to your target market

- And more: Airports, marinas, boat yards, yacht clubs, theaters, schools, dance studios, marital arts facilities, car repair, therapists, basically any business that shares your target market in area, situation, or type of property.

A good way to get this started is to make a list. Save it so you can add to it over time. Think about all the businesses that someone you have decided is your ideal client would use in their normal course of business and daily life.

If you have decided on an area, then start with all the businesses in that area. Then go through them and rate them how connected they would be to people in that area. The top businesses to share your target market should be the first ones you work on. Like local markets for instance. Businesses that someone would visit because of the proximity to the homes there.

If you have decided on a situation, then start with all the businesses that someone in that situation would be using at the same time. Go through and rate them and then target the top ones for building relationships with.

And, if you have decided on a type of property, then start with the businesses that share this target market. Then just go through these and start with the top ones. Example would be for vacation rentals, you would target cleaning companies, property management companies, interior decorators, local and national travel magazines, restaurants, car rental companies, etc. In other words, who would the owner rely on, but also who the tenants would need as well. The point is to identify businesses and people who interact with your target market.

But it doesn't stop there. Once you have some businesses who cater to your clients, then you can start promoting these businesses to your clients. Human nature is predictable. When you refer people to an attorney, and they know you well, they will refer you clients as well. Additionally, if you partner on marketing efforts, then they will know and like you, and naturally they will refer you. And finally, when you demonstrate that you handle their referrals really well, they will hear about it (as in feedback from the referral) which will help reinforce the action in the first place.

An example would be for a local restaurant that is child-friendly, and let's say you help new families buy a larger home and sell their current one. You get to know the owner and manager of the restaurant and you book the place once a month for your "new families home buying workshop" hosted by the restaurant, they should be happy as you are helping get people in the door. Make sure to tell the owner and manager that you plan on doing this once a month consistently, and that you will be advertising it on the radio and local paper.

This is a very simple way to work with businesses to show them you are a professional and very serious about your success. You should even negotiate having your booklet upfront for people to look at while they wait for a table.

Some key points: Any person or business you work with like this should be clean, honest, and have a very good reputation for treating their customers well. Also, you need to have a good rapport with them. Next, remember to give first, then let them reciprocate. Meaning, help them get clients first before asking for them to refer you. Become friends first. Use them for your own needs if possible. Don't just take, make sure to give much to them and you will be seen as someone they can refer out.

If you just call up local businesses and ask if they will refer you leads, then you'll find out quickly that they won't. You will waste your time and offend them to the point of them never referring you any business. Finally, make sure that if you host any educational event make it open to the public – all are welcome. You don't want to pre-screen anyone – even if you target seniors, and a young family shows up, just smile and be happy they're there. And along with this is no discounts can be offered to your clients and vice versa. Recommendations are fine, but monetization is not. No coupons, special invites, discounts, bonus service or product, etc. You should never incentivize anything. Just provide honest, genuine help free of any strings attached.

Quick summary: Having a team of other agents to support your incoming leads and marketing efforts will be very helpful! Also, having many local businesses and influential people who you know and trust, and who know you and can recommend you, will help funnel prospects to you year-round. More on how to do that next.

PART FOUR: YOUR "BACK END"

No, not your behind, your back-end marketing. Here is what I mean:

What happens AFTER the deal closes? For most agents, they just move on struggling to find the next deal.

But you should now realize how valuable the relationship is that you've built. You should not let that wither and die; you should keep in touch.

Why would you want to keep in touch with your past clients, local businesses that share your target market, or even other agents? Well, it's so they can all point prospects to you. If you were just a generic agent with no specialty, then there are plenty of those around. But since you're an expert at a certain type of transaction, property, area, etc. then they will naturally think of you first. The more you stand out, and the more contacts you have, then the more people will know you as the expert.

"Build your backend" means to have some follow up. That is, stay in touch, keep building on the relationship. Then think about what else can you provide your customers to make them coming back to you again and again, and especially what additional services can you recommend and even provide to them yourself?

The point is to keep building the relationship further. You can do this in many ways of course, but here are some suggestions:

•   Clients that you've built a relationship with: Email, call, or mail a card to them at least twice a year. In this communication can be your recommendation for various businesses and services that may be of some real help to them. Obviously, these are businesses that you have used and can vouch for and are probably ones that you've built relationships with already. If you can, try to take your previous clients to lunch once a year. Just doing this can provide you with new leads every week.

•   Other RE agents that you've built relationships with: This can range from a lunch every month, to you running a referral group twice a month, or even talking every few days on the phone. It just depends on the connection and understanding you've built with them. You could even offer to partner with them in some of the ideas you've learned in this book.

• 3rd party businesses and service providers that share your target market: First, at every chance you get, use them for your own needs. Second, make a point of speaking with them in person or at least on the phone every month at a minimum. Ask them about their business and what they see as new innovations, new ideas, new marketing plans they may have, etc. People love to talk about themselves and being a good listener can instantly improve how they view you. Ask them questions about their business and be genuinely interested.

A back-end marketing system is a scheduled follow up plan.

So, come up with:

• How you will keep building the relationships further.

• How often you'll do this.

• Then schedule it. Don't assume that you will just do it, you need to put it on your calendar.

Next, start thinking of what else you can provide to your clients. Part of this was mentioned previously, about referring a business to your prospects. This can extend to moving companies, painters, cleaning services, and even dentists, tax accountants, etc. As long as you are honestly referring a quality service to your clients, for free, then you are doing them a service. Again, no discounts or kickbacks should be considered. Just honest recommendations.

Quick summary: Why would you stop interacting with your clients once the escrow closes? You worked hard to get their property sold, or bought, or rented – so why stop there? Keep building the relationship and keep in touch!

Final Note: Always check with your broker and your State Governing Agency or Department for guidelines on business referrals – you do not want to violate RESPA – so always check!

WHERE TO GO FROM HERE

I hope you've found this book worthwhile. I strongly believe that if you just follow the steps and take action consistently, then you will see fast results.

To help you with putting all this into action, I have created a workbook and video series that guides you through the steps outlined in the book and is a basic "fill-in-the-blank" tool to help you.

Download a copy of the workbook and get the videos delivered via email by entering your best email address at this site: BetterAgentAcademy.com

It's FREE to you as a reader of this book.

ABOUT THE AUTHOR

Will Cunningham has worked in Real Estate lending since 1993, closed thousands of transactions, and helped hundreds of Real Estate agents get quality financing for their clients. Will has held his RE Broker's License in California since 2002.

Thank you for reading HOW TO DOMINATE YOUR MARKET IN ONE YEAR OR LESS *FOR REAL ESTATE AGENTS ONLY - *4 STEPS TO CREATE AN AUTOMATIC SUPPLY OF NEW LEADS COMING IN WEEK AFTER WEEK* Contact Will by visiting: BetterAgentAcademy.com

www.ingramcontent.com/pod-product-compliance
Lightning Source LLC
Chambersburg PA
CBHW021513210526
45463CB00002B/1002